Marion
Hilliard

Mary Carol Wilson

WINGHAM BRANCH LIBRARY

Fitzhenry & Whiteside Limited

Contents

The Author

Mary Carol Wilson is a professional author who has written on subjects ranging from art to business. She is a past national president of the Canadian Authors' Association.

© 1977, Fitzhenry and Whiteside Limited
150 Lesmill Road,
Don Mills, Ont. M3B 2T5

Printed and bound in Canada

ISBN 0-88902-215-1

Glorious Chapter 1
Childhood

Blonde, blue-eyed Marion Hilliard was born on June 17, 1902 in the St. Lawrence river town of Morrisburg, Ontario. She was born into a happy household and a pious one. Her parents, Anna and Irwin Hilliard, were of mixed Irish and English descent. They were staunch, missionary-minded Methodists, highly respected in the community, active in village affairs and in their church. Their first home, where Marion was born, was named Piety Cottage.

Piety Cottage, Morrisburg

The town of Morrisburg was a bustling place. It had originated as a trading post for the shipment of logs down the river to be made into masts for the shipbuilding industry. Its founders had emigrated first to the United States, then to Canada, to join the United Empire Loyalists at the time of the American Revolution. River-front lots had been granted to these settlers and through their own hard work they had prospered. Their children still took pride in being descended from men who had fought and repelled the American army at Crysler's Farm on November 11, 1813. Now this peaceful community loaded produce such as grain, fine quality butter and McIntosh apples onto the river boats instead of logs.

Irwin Hilliard was a lawyer, and a stern but fair man. He had a busy practice and his legal judgement was highly regarded. Anna Hilliard, ten years younger than her husband, was a vital, enthusiastic woman with a sense of eagerness about life which she passed on to all her children. She was the first child of a family of eight, while Irwin was the eighth child of a family of eleven. The Hilliard household abounded in uncles, aunts and cousins who came to visit or wrote newsy letters from faraway places.

Marion was the third child in a family which grew to five. Foster was the eldest, Ruth the second child and after Marion came Helen Barbara, then Irwin.

In spite of many duties which took Mr. and Mrs.

Ruth, Marion, and Foster

What sort of education was generally thought suitable for young girls in the early part of this century? What was it supposed to prepare them for?

Hilliard away from home, concern for their children's well-being and happiness was uppermost in their minds. Anna Hilliard insisted that her daughters have the same education as was provided for her sons — a somewhat uncommon attitude in the early part of the century. Marion, in particular, loved school, and was always one of the top three in her class. Piano lessons for each of the Hilliard children began at age five and often, until two pianos were acquired, one child would practice every day at a neighbour's.

Though in later years Marion always referred to her childhood as "those glorious years," she had some small fears and disappointments. She was terrified of thunder storms and used to huddle on the sofa with her head covered, while Helen Barbara hid in the clothes closet. She was also afraid of the dark.

All the Hilliard children had some daily duties, and one of Marion's was the task of brushing bugs off the potato vines. She shuddered every time she had to do it. Another of her tasks was to bring Daisy, the stubborn family cow, from the pasture each evening to be milked. Not only did Marion fear the dark, she was also slightly afraid of Daisy. She tried very hard to exchange duties with another member of the family or even to get some-one to accompany her, but without success. She soon found that the best thing to do was to get the job over with as quickly as possible.

If there was a lot of work, there was a lot of play, too. A favourite playground for the Hilliard children was the big barn which stood behind Oak Hall, a larger house into which they moved as the family grew. The barn was usually occupied by a sleek black horse named Tommy Kay, a flock of chickens and, sometimes, by Daisy the cow. There were also a surrey, a buggy and two cutters, the last being stored on the rafters during the summer.

What is a surrey? A cutter?

The Hilliard children discovered that dust covers from the cutters made ideal stage curtains, and they used them in the shows they and their friends put on for the whole neighbourhood. Two cents was the price of admission and all proceeds went to the church mission band. Songs, acrobatics and playlets were all produced, directed and acted by nine-year-old Marion with the help of her best friends. Ladders across the beams made trapezes. When costumes were needed the girls raided the attic of the house for Mrs. Hilliard's old dresses and hats.

Parents in the audience smiled and clapped as they listened to songs like "Down by the Old Mill Stream" or "Row, Row Your Boat." Later they held their breaths while their offspring "skinned the cat" and clambered over the trapezes. But Marion was a careful organizer. No accidents were reported.

Marion at age 16

What happens at a Camp Meeting?

At quieter times, Marion and her friend Marjorie stayed on the porch and played house. Marion told everyone her ambition was to be "a married lady with six children."

The front lawn of the Hilliard house made a croquet lawn or tennis court in summer, and in winter, a skating rink used by all the children in the neighbourhood. Marion learned to skate soon after she learned to walk. She became more and more proficient as the years went by, and longed to play hockey with the boys. They would have none of her. Nothing daunted, Marion sat on the puck so no one could play until her mother was called upon to arbitrate. Finally, because Marion could skate with the best of them, she was allowed to join the team.

Like all Morrisburg children, Marion learned to swim and row a boat at an early age. When Marion's father built a summer cottage in a pine grove at Iroquois Point, twelve kilometres up the river, Marion was overjoyed at the possibilities of endless swimming and boating. The cottage was named Irwanna, a combination of the parents' first names. When school was out for the summer, the family travelled by wagon to the cottage, carrying with them the piano and other necessities. Foster, the eldest son, followed on foot, leading Daisy, the cow.

Irwanna was crowded to the rafters all summer long. Many relatives and friends came to visit and to attend the Methodist Camp Meeting which took place nearby.

"Last one in has to do the dishes!" was the cry each morning as the children tumbled out of bed, pulled on their bathing suits and raced to the river bank. They all loved the water. Each child had to prove he or she was a strong swimmer before being allowed to clamber down the rocks to the thrilling swiftness of the river on one side of the point. When prowess had been proven, the swimmers then dared to go farther and ride the swells from the excursion boats plying between Cornwall and Kingston.

During summers at Irwanna, the river was an integral part of every activity. Each day one of the teenagers was elected to row Mrs. Hilliard on her daily fishing expedition, which provided the family dinner. The days were a busy round of worship, chores and sports, all

A Hilliard gathering at Irwanna, 1911

carried on close to the water. When night came, all were
lulled to sleep by the murmur of the river and the
soughing of the wind in the pines.

When autumn came and the family moved back to
Morrisburg, Mrs. Hilliard was frequently called away
from home on her church work. In order to keep the
household going, there was always help of one kind
or another in the home. Many teenage relatives from the
country would come for a year or two to enable them to
attend school in Morrisburg. They would live at Oak Hall
and help with the housework in exchange for room and
board. Gradually however, Marion and the other children took over many of the household duties, learning
to cook, make beds and clean. The elder ones also helped
look after the younger children.

Marion loved looking after her baby brother, Irwin.
He was her favourite. One autumn during the annual
Fall Fair she dressed him in his best and entered him
in the baby contest without telling anyone. She sat

Typical of the regimen of girls' schools in the 1920s was this gym class at Havergal College, Toronto

Marion with her brother, Irwin

proudly with the rather frail child on her knee, and was bitterly disappointed when the judges passed him over.

The anxious years of the Great War disrupted the happy, peaceful life of the Hilliard household. Marion's older brother Foster, then at university, enlisted and spent three years in the army.

What were battle conditions like in World War I? Why were there such deep feelings about them? Try to find some of Seigfried Sassoon's poetry about that war.

Fourteen-year-old Marion's contribution to the war effort was to work on a farm during the summer. One day she was asked to skin two rabbits for supper. Later, when she told an older friend what fun she had found this to be, the friend asked if she had ever thought of becoming a doctor.

"Yes," Marion replied, "but I don't think my parents would let me."

"You will if you really want to," her friend said.

A few years later Marion was studying hard for her Grade 13 examinations. She was also preparing to try her senior piano examination. She wanted to be a concert pianist. She made Grade 13 with honours, but, to her bitter disappointment, failed in music. She told the family she wanted to try the examination again. Her father said, "If you can't be the best, forget it." She didn't take the examination.

What do you think of the statement "If you can't be the best, forget it"?

Marion was ready for university. Her interests started to turn in other directions.

Chapter 2 **Lady of Letters**

Marion registered at Victoria College, University of Toronto, in September of 1920. Her father insisted she was to become a teacher — a sensible career for a woman. After a furious argument with him she won his permission to study science — his understanding being that eventually she would teach science rather than practise it.

Marion and her roommates at college — Izzy, Betty and Maryon — shared quarters in which there was barely room to 'swing a cat.' That didn't matter to them. They shared their boxes of food from home, discussed their studies, swapped news of sports scores and parties and generally had a good time together. Because Marion and Maryon were always getting mixed up because of their similar names, they soon became known around Victoria College as Hilliard and Moody.

In her first winter at college, Marion skated every chance she got at the college rink. The Little Vic Band would play in the evenings, so right after dinner she and her three roommates rushed into the frosty air, skates in hand. The combination of music, rhythmic motion and ozone was one of Marion's great pleasures.

There were so many things to do in Toronto, some of which had formerly been denied in Marion's strict upbringing. While still retaining the utmost respect for the opinions of her parents, Marion felt free for the first time in her life to try such so-called frivolous things as dancing, cards and the theatre. Her older brother, Foster, was again at university, and he introduced her to concerts such as she had never heard before. Her love of music was fed by the Mendelssohn Choir, symphony concerts, opera, and recitals by such famous artists as Louise Homer. Her roommates' parents came to the city occasionally, and would take the girls to shows.

Marion's science courses were tough, requiring long lab sessions and much study at weekends. This made it difficult for her, as she loved the literary society, the glee club and all sports. But Marion soon established a pattern for her college life. She spent lots of time on

C. H. Best and F. G. Banting, 1921

all her extra-curricular activities for most of the school year. But six weeks before examinations in May, she forgot everything but her studies. She called it "submerging." That way she managed to have lots of fun, and yet passed creditably each year.

In the winter of 1921-2, an event of importance made a great impression on Marion. It was the epoch-making medical discovery by Doctors Banting and Best of the benefits of insulin in treating diabetes.

How was diabetes treated before the discovery of insulin treatment? What prize was awarded to the scientists who discovered insulin treatment?

Though Marion maintained a good academic record, where she really made her mark at college was in sports. Marion was the star of the Varsity Girls Hockey Team. Her speed on the ice and her expert stick handling made her the darling of the spectators. In spring, on the tennis courts, she put to use the experience gained on the family court in Morrisburg and startled her opponents with her smashing serves. But of all sports, hockey remained her first love.

In her third year, after a spectacular Varsity victory over the McGill hockey team, Marion was named Athlete of the Year. It was a proud moment when she was

The University of Toronto's championship hockey team, 1925. Marion is at lower left.

presented with the hallowed hockey stick, engraved in silver with the names of previous winners. She won Vic's Vs for performance on the college volleyball, basketball and hockey teams as well as the Varsity Vs in ice hockey and tennis. She became known in Varsity circles as the "lady of letters."

What is the Student Christian Movement? Is the SCM still active today?

For all her enjoyment of these extra-curricular activities, perhaps the strongest influence on Marion's future was her interest in the Student Christian Movement. The shocking war experiences of servicemen who had returned to university led many students to seriously examine their religious beliefs. Some churchmen worried that the SCM was leading students to 'doubt' at a time when their faith needed strengthening. But the students longed for a new depth of religion, something more than what they felt to be the stale beliefs of their parents. The war had opened their eyes to "man's inhumanity to man."

Marion served as president of the SCM for several years and each fall attended their annual meetings at Elgin House in Muskoka. "I am a child of God," she told a friend. She retained this conviction all her life.

Sir William Osler was a famous Canadian physician. Find out something about his work.

There was no serious or lasting romance in Marion's life at this time, although she was popular with the boys as a fine athlete with an infectious laugh and a real sense of fun. She enjoyed vicariously the romance of her best friend Maryon Moody. A young professor at the college, Mike Pearson, had fallen in love with Maryon, and just before graduation they became engaged with Marion's wholehearted approval. A year later it was a great thrill for Marion to travel by train to Winnipeg and act as maid of honour at the wedding of Maryon and Mike. Later, Marion was godmother to the first Pearson child.

Graduating with a Bachelor of Arts degree in 1924, Marion was still determined to study medicine, much to the dismay of her father. That autumn found her back on campus with a Moss Scholarship. Hard work was ahead of her, but she took as a motto a quotation from Sir William Osler's writings which she copied and kept among her papers.

Work is the open sesame to every portal, the great equalizer of the world, the true philosopher's stone that transmutes all the base metal of humanity into gold. The stupid man among you it makes bright; the bright man brilliant and the brilliant . . . steady.

*The miracles of life are in it. The blind see by touch, the dumb
speak with fingers. To the youth it brings hope, to the middle-aged
confidence, to the aged repose. True balm of hurt minds, in its
presence the heart of the sorrowful is lightened and consoled.*

It was only in 1906 that the University of Toronto
Medical School had finally opened its doors to women.
At first they were barely tolerated. Back in the 1870s
two women, Emily Stowe and Jennie Trout, had been
allowed to attend lectures provided they would make no
fuss, whatever happened. What did happen was that the
male students so resented their presence they covered

*When were women admitted
to other courses or
professional studies such as
law and engineering in
Canadian universities? Are
women barred from any
fields of study in Canada
today?*

*The wedding of Maryon
Moody and Lester Pearson*

Why did the lecturers and male students resent the presence of women? What do you think of their attitudes?

the walls with deliberately disgusting sketches. Many needless objectionable stories were told by lecturers while the boys watched for the girls' reaction. Finally one of the girls said she would tell a lecturer's wife exactly what he had said and after that the persecution eased. Now, in the twenties, the Medettes, as female Meds were then called, were fairly lucky. There was no difficulty about their being allowed to attend all classes and clinics. "Of course," Marion later wrote, "the girls had to sit in the front row and you could hardly say we were welcome — but we certainly were not outcasts."

But despite her high resolve, Marion shortly faltered in her determination to become a doctor. During her early clinical work she was shocked at the suffering she saw and conditions she had never encountered in her sheltered life. To witness the pain of another human being which often could not be alleviated hurt her deeply. The smell of unwashed bodies and the sight of acute alcoholism disgusted her. Never would she forget the harrowing experience of seeing a patient actually turn blue and die before her eyes.

After a few months she reported to her father, "I can't stand it! I think I'll have to leave medicine." He was appalled and this time it was he who was adamant.

What is your opinion of her father's advice to Marion?

"Nothing of the kind," he said. "Finish what you started. Be a doctor!"

Shortly after this Marion was in the delivery room, for the first time watching a baby being born. There was the mother, her face wet with tears. The tense concentration of the doctor and nurses was riveted on the moment of birth. Then came the cry of the baby with its first breath. Within Marion a flash of insight arose — this was what life was all about. That day she made her final decision. She would become an obstetrician.

In her last year of study, Marion became a junior intern at the Women's College Hospital. She attended the staff doctor on rounds, took the case histories of new patients, wrote orders, was responsible for starting intravenous feedings, administered medicines, and had many other duties. She did them all efficiently. Her chief soon recognized her as being very conscientious. Nevertheless, that same chief wrote in a report: "Bouncy . . . might need holding down."

Find out more about the working conditions and salaries of nurses in the 1920s. How do they compare with today's?

Off-duty, Marion still participated in active sports.

She tried to encourage some of the nurses to do so as well. She was worried about the long hours the nurses spent on duty. The effects showed in their tired appearance. She shocked the senior staff by appearing in the lounge one day dressed in gym bloomers and carrying a ukelele. Undaunted, she called the nurses to come and have some fun. Soon after, she made arrangements for them to swim at the Y.W.C.A. and organized Sunday evening singsongs.

Within a short while, the hospital superintendent was surprised to notice how much more energetic her nurses seemed to be and how much happier in their work. It did not seem possible that this had been accomplished by a little recreation, but young Marion proved it to be so.

Eventually, a more reasonable schedule of hours for the nurses was arranged. And throughout her career, Marion always made it a practice to keep a watchful eye on the nursing staff and interns in the hospital.

Finally in 1927, the momentous day arrived. Marion knelt before the Chancellor of the University in Convocation Hall and received the hood of Bachelor of Medicine. The big question was: what to do next? More than anything else, she wanted to be an obstetrician. But this would require a year's internship in that particular field. There was also the difficulty of getting a good internship in competition with the male graduates. She was very conscious that she had been a drain on the family budget during her seven years of study. What about going to India? Should she fulfill her mother's hope that she become a missionary? Again it was found that she should have some postgraduate work first.

Wise counselling by some of her instructors sparked another idea in Marion's mind. If somehow she could take a postgraduate course in obstetrics in a London hospital and pass her examinations there, this would give her prestige in establishing a practice later in Toronto. Now, all that was needed was money. This was loaned to her by a well-to-do older woman whom she considered her "fairy godmother."

Marion went happily home to Morrisburg to spend some time with her parents and to help with preparations for the wedding of her sister, Ruth. Just twenty-four hours after seeing the bridal couple off on their honeymoon, Marion left for England.

Marion's graduation portrait

What are the qualifications for missionaries and what tasks do they perform?

Chapter 3 **Study Abroad**

Marion's eight day voyage on the *Empress of Australia* was for her a time of introspection. Although she occupied a cabin with three other people, they were strangers to her. For the first time in her life she was lonely. She felt very far away from her family and friends. She resolved: "One thing I shall learn from this trip — poise. I'm not used to being absolutely on my own."

The first part of the voyage was a little rough. Unlike most of the passengers, Marion managed to avoid 'mal de mer' by frantically walking the deck and spending as much time as possible in the open air. Besides, she couldn't bear to miss a meal. When the deck became more steady, she began to enjoy shuffleboard with some other students on board. She wrote home that after having had a good rest she was now feeling 'spry as a kitten.'

One of her adventures into sophistication was betting 25¢ on a white wooden horse. She won $4.10. Stricken by the thought of how shocked the members of her home church would be at such depravity she paid her respects to them and salved her own conscience by betting her winnings until all were lost.

After a pleasant voyage, the *Empress of Australia* docked at Southampton on July 13th. Marion travelled by train to London where she searched in vain for her luggage and a friend of a friend who was supposed to meet her. It made for a depressing arrival. The friend of a friend never appeared, but her luggage was finally located, and a shipboard acquaintance helped her find a room at Bailey's Hotel.

So it was with a mixture of apprehension and excitement that Marion spent her first night in the vast city of London. It seemed such a contrast to the peaceful life aboard ship. That evening she wrote to her parents: "Woe's me, this being a woman of the world has its worries."

Marion had been asked by the Canadian Branch of the

Student Christian Movement to represent them at conferences in England and in Switzerland, so her first duty was to report to the headquarters in Swanwick. Here she met Margaret Read, the National Secretary of SCM and another Canadian, Marion Wrong. When they found out she was "operating on a shoestring," they offered her a job as cook in their London home in exchange for room and board. Marion was happy about this arrangement — her budget would now stretch a little farther. It was a job she could easily handle after her early training at home.

She spent ten days exploring the city of London. She registered at Canada House, where she devoured the Toronto papers and met many visiting Canadians. She enjoyed the parks in London, particularly Kensington Gardens, where she fell in love with the whimsical statue of Peter Pan. Later on this became a place of refuge for her in times of stress.

Then she set off for the conference in Switzerland, stopping in Paris enroute. Marion had been fascinated by London, but Paris simply intoxicated her, even without wine. Switzerland was delightful, and she was very proud to represent Canada at the conference. She deeply believed in the aims of the movement, which included the promotion of international goodwill and became much admired for her outspoken contribution to discussion. She was quickly appointed the conference doctor. She ended up treating lots of colds and cases of indigestion caused by the delicious food served at mealtimes.

On the last night of the conference, the delegates were entertained by the citizens of Schiers. Marion described it in a letter to her parents.

"Peter Pan" in Kensington Gardens

"We were all in a conference meeting when we heard the cannon go off and we dashed off to the top of a nearby hill. We were hurrying along a goat path when I raised my head and bang, the cannon went off again and I thought I was shot. So we climbed above the gun and above the fires. I do wish you could have seen it — fires blazing on all the hills and the moon shining on the snow-capped mountains. As we stood there, all the children from the village came along, each carrying a lighted lantern, and they wound along the road singing. I never hope to see anything more wonderful in such white moonlight."

After an hilarious and very inexpensive 15-day tour of Europe with a group of friends made at the conference, Marion returned to London and her job as part-time cook. She liked the white, gabled house in Golder's Green and her little room, with, joy of joys, a fireplace all her own. She quickly unpacked her bags and settled in.

Her days were carefully planned. She was the first one up in the mornings, and prepared breakfast for herself, Margaret and the other Marion. She served a seven o'clock dinner each evening, having shopped for groceries on her way home from hospital or clinic. A charwoman came regularly to clean the house and it all worked beautifully. Her employers introduced her to their friends, respected her study periods and were careful not to impose on her.

Marion's first letter of introduction in the medical field was presented to a tiny, red-haired woman who looked like a fashionable member of the aristocracy. She was Miss Gertrude Dearnley, a brilliant gynecological surgeon who promptly took Marion under her wing, supervised her studies, and became a lifelong friend.

Gertrude Dearnley with Marion at Miss Dearnley's cottage in Surrey

Marion found that in England, surgeons rarely used the title of Doctor. She also learned that here there was full equality for women in the field of medicine, something that was sadly lacking in Canada. This heightened her determination to prove that she, as a Canadian woman doctor, could attain the highest standing in her profession. Here Miss Dearnley was of great help in arranging her acceptance for courses of study under the most expert people available.

She chose first a six months' clinical assistantship in the Hospital for Women in Soho Square. She also started a series of surgical tutorials with the head of surgery at the Royal Free Hospital where Miss Dearnley operated. She was both amazed and awed to witness the speed and efficiency of this tiny woman in the operating room.

Marion's studies included the handling of septic abortions, and work on sterility about which she was most enthusiastic. In October she sat for her written and oral examinations, earning her degree of Licentiate, Royal College of Physicians.

When Christmas came, Marion was very depressed. It was her first Christmas away from home and mail from Canada was delayed until early in the New Year. She was so low in spirits that on Christmas Eve she cried over a bunch of holly.

Next morning she attended service at Southwark Cathedral, then braced herself to cook a Christmas dinner for a party of six. The turkey, potatoes, artichokes, cranberry sauce, fruit salad, plum pudding with hard sauce and salted almonds brought lavish compliments for the cook. That cheered her up a little, and in the evening it began to snow, which made the best part of the day for homesick Marion.

In January she became the third Canadian woman to be granted the degree of Member of the Royal College of Surgeons. Her six months' service as cook was over, and she moved into residence at the Queen Charlotte Hospital for a course in midwifery. At first life seemed rather luxurious — she had a private room and maid service. But Marion soon found that she was on the run for the full four weeks of her course. How she loved it! This was the work which interested her most. She became known to the surgeon in charge as "Miss Canada," and soon she was handling cases she "wouldn't have

QUALIFICATION TO PRACTISE MEDICINE, SURGERY, AND MIDWIFERY.

I John Rose Bradford, K.C.M.G. M.D.
President of the Royal College of Physicians of
London, with the consent of the Fellows of the same
College, have under the authority given to us by
Royal Charter and Act of Parliament, granted to

Anna Marion Hilliard

who has satisfied the College of her proficiency, our Licence
under the said Charter to practise Physic, including therein
the practice of Medicine, Surgery, and Midwifery, so long
as she shall continue to obey the Statutes, Bye-Laws, and
Regulations of the College relating to Licentiates, in witness
whereof we have this day set our Seal and Signatures.
Dated at the College the twenty-sixth day of January
in the year of our Lord, one thousand, nine hundred
and twenty eight

John Rose Bradford President.

EXAMINERS.

P. Horton Smith Hartley M.D.	Eardley Holland F.R.C.S
Charlton Briscoe M.D	Donald R. Ry F.R.S
James C. Toveus M.D	Malcolm Donaldson F.R.C.S.
Frederick Langmead M.D.	Trevor B Davies F.R.C.S

I Certify that Anna Marion Hilliard   to whom this Licence has
been granted by the College, and whose Signature is subjoined has been duly admitted
to practise Physic as a Licentiate of the College, and that such Licence is a Legal authority
to her to practise Medicine, Surgery, and Midwifery, and to dispense Medicines, but only
to those who are her own patients.

Licentiate Anna Marion Hilliard   Registrar Raymond Crawfurd M.D.

believed possible a month ago." Her certificate read that she had attended 92 cases of labour in four weeks and had assisted at various obstetrical operations.

From the Queen Charlotte, Marion moved to a Salvation Army Hospital known as "The Mothers'." It made quite a contrast to the luxury of the Queen Charlotte. She occupied a bleak little room, and there was no maid to run her bath water or make tea. At the Queen Charlotte, she had been the only woman at a table with nine male interns. Here, she was served her meals in isolation behind a screen in the dining room, quite separate from the Army personnel, all women bearing various ranks such as Captain or Adjutant. Nevertheless, she respected the Army people and their religion, and found little intolerance. At first the Army people were a bit cold because they thought Marion came from the United States — a nation not much respected by the English at that time. But this was soon overcome, and her diary recorded that she was now used to coming into new places and did not think she would ever be really lonesome again. She sailed through the course quite happily before moving on to Dublin for the next stage of her education.

Opposite:
Marion's certificate from the
Royal College of Physicians

The Salvation Army was
quite a controversial
institution in its early days.
Find out more about the
origins of this movement.
George Bernard Shaw's play,
Major Barbara, contains
some interesting ideas about
the Army's philosophy.

Queen Charlotte Hospital

At the Rotunda Hospital in Dublin she was again on call all night and a new experience for her was to go out in partnership with a male intern to do home deliveries. Other students teased her about running off at night with a man, which highly amused her.

Marion felt that some parts of Dublin fairly "shrieked of human misery," when she visited the squalid homes in various slum areas. Often she found that there were already ten or twelve children in the family and little or no preparation made for a new baby. She was amazed at the sturdy physiques of many of the mothers in spite of their poverty and concluded, "I guess it must be my Irish ancestry that makes me so hardy."

She came to enjoy the Irish people and their delightful speech. When she had an opportunity to travel through the countryside she was enthralled with the beauty of flowering hedges along roads leading down to the sea. Returning from one such excursion she wrote, "No matter how dull life may become, for a few hours I lived in a fairy tale."

In between clinics, lectures, church and the night calls, Marion began to play tennis each day. Her first invitation to play came from a male intern who fancied

The Rotunda Hospital, Dublin

himself an expert. He must have been taken down a peg when Marion beat him six-one, six-one and six-love. Other players proved themselves more worthy opponents and the sport kept them all in fit condition.

Marion was taken off the home delivery team after her 21st case in just three weeks. She wrote home, "I surely have enjoyed myself here."

Her studies abroad were complete. She began to make plans to return home. First she travelled by freighter to Plymouth. Miss Dearnley had invited her to spend a last holiday there. Marion landed with only one shilling in her purse but she was met on the pier and well looked after by her hostess.

It was here that Marion celebrated her 26th birthday, in the midst of what seemed to her many little luxuries, including delicious food, to which she was addicted. Knowing Marion's love for tennis, Miss Dearnley took her guest to an exclusive club to play. When they arrived, Marion found she had brought two left tennis shoes. Many years later she wrote, "It never crossed my mind to make some excuse or try to borrow a pair of shoes. I joyfully bounced out on the court in my two left shoes and played with my usual uninhibited style. The women doctors who watched my strange-gaited footwork have never forgotten me."

Marion drove back to London with a friend, visiting Stonehenge enroute, then began a round of farewells and shopping for gifts. On July 7 she boarded the *Empress of Scotland* for the trip home. It was a year and a day since she had left Canada.

"Low in my mind when on board," her diary records. Then she began to think how wonderful it would be "to have the fun of doing things rather than still learning out of books." She wondered how long it would be before she had a "real, honest to goodness patient of my own."

Marion Hilliard, "woman of the world"

Chapter 4 Homecoming and Private Practice

It was glorious to be home again in the midst of a joyful family reunion. Parents, brothers, sisters, uncles, aunts and cousins all came to spend the summer at Irwanna and to welcome Marion home. And Marion herself realized all the more how much she had missed her family and the sound of the river.

In autumn Marion set out for Toronto, "to seek her fortune," as she said. Here she was warmly welcomed by Mike and Maryon Pearson with their son, her godchild. They planned a wonderful winter together, but this was not to be. Mike was offered his first job with the Department of External Affairs in Ottawa and the Pearsons moved there not long after their reunion with Marion.

Marion decided to set up a general practice in the Physicians and Surgeons Building. She resolved to accept patients as they came, promising herself that she would specialize in obstetrics and gynecology only when she could afford it. She was also accepted as a welcome addition to the obstetrical staff at Womens College Hospital on Rusholme Road, where she had served earlier as a junior intern.

For some time Marion's office was "remarkably uncluttered with patients," but she already knew what it meant to be poor. And a young woman doctor friend had warned her that the financial rewards for straight medical practice were apt to be very slim at first. In her own practice she had taken in eight dollars and fifty cents in her first month and the sum of fifty-nine dollars in the last month of her first year. Expenses included not only rent but the fees of the Ontario Medical Association.

Marion filled in the time by writing long letters to her family and friends. She also decided to try her hand at

Who belongs to the Ontario Medical Association? What services does it perform for its members?

writing mystery stories, but there is no record of their acceptance for publication.

Some of her night calls were harrowing experiences. She wrote to a friend:

"Bundling myself in my warmest clothes, I climbed on the streetcar at three in the morning with my satchel of instruments and a map of the city. Though I have had a lifelong fear of the dark, I found the house and stood my ground while a police dog leaped and barked around me. I discovered my patient was in an advanced state of delirium tremens. She died a few minutes after I arrived.

"The second one was to another remote and shabby neighbourhood, this one happily devoid of watchdogs. The patient was again unconscious, this time suffering from toxemia, and she died a few minutes after my arrival. The third night call was no different. This patient was an old woman with uremia. Like the others she was unconscious when I reached her and died a few minutes later.

"Luckily for my confidence, as well as for my patients, my next cases survived."

During her struggle to establish herself, Marion took on various sidelines. She was the first doctor appointed to the Children's Aid Society, where she obtained an insight into many social problems. As in her student

Toronto slums

days, she was shaken by some of the appalling conditions she encountered — the filthy homes and neglected or mistreated children. She realized how badly her help was needed and she gave it freely. She truly loved the children and teenagers who were referred to her, and they found her the kind of person to whom they could spill out their problems.

Soon Marion was called upon to speak to church and school groups on health subjects. She charged $5.00 for each lecture. She was one of the first doctors to speak openly on sex education and was especially skillful in dealing with male-female relationships in a matter-of-fact way that caused little or no embarrassment.

Marion was not a person whose morals were shaped by convention. She never condoned premarital sex, but

A pre-school clinic in the 1920s

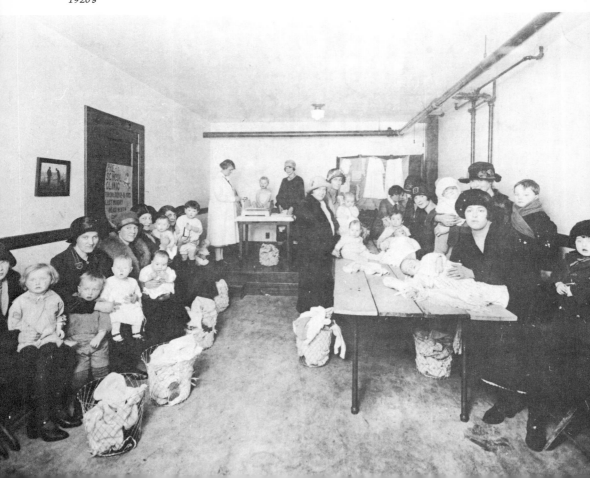

neither did she condemn it. "Each act is followed, without fail, by a consequence," she said. She felt strongly that young people must learn to make decisions themselves, bolstered by the discipline that comes of appreciating the consequences.

"A person's life is sorted out in airtight compartments; a time for being born, a time for dying; a time for loving and a time for learning. This is your time for learning, the only time you will get until you die. On your learning depends your knowledge and on your knowledge depends your career, your marriage . . . and the wisdom that will direct your life. These years of learning are too important to be overwhelmed by passions. Put education

What do you think of Marion's statement: "These years of learning are too important to be overwhelmed by passion"?

A travelling clinic in rural Alberta in the 1920s

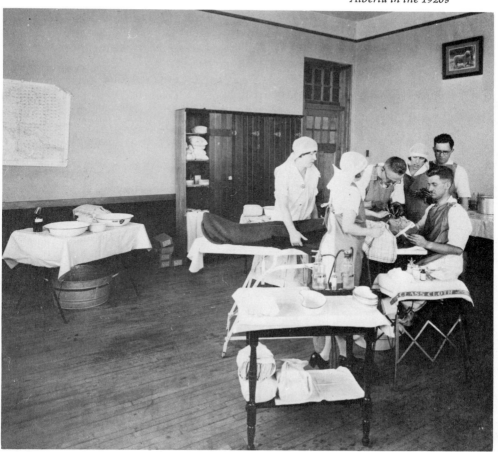

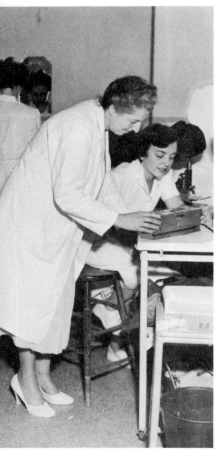

Dr. Eva Mader McDonald in a Women's College Hospital laboratory in the 1950s

first just now; afterwards you will have fifty years left for loving."

Later Marion became the medical examiner at the Y.W.C.A., at a fee of 50¢ per examination. This job, her work at Children's Aid and her lectures helped to pay her office expenses and her room in a private boarding house. She was also saving to pay back the loan which had financed her studies abroad. It was a difficult time, but Marion held onto her hopes for the future.

In 1929 a new friend appeared on the scene. She was Dr. Eva Mader, (later Dr. Eva Mader McDonald, a chancellor of the University of Toronto). Both she and Marion were living in boarding houses, but in the following year they decided to join forces and not only share an office but rent a flat of their own. They found an attic on St. Mary's Street with two rooms, kitchen and bath at thirty-five dollars a month. This was just within their budget and the location suited them very well.

The flat had a fireplace and casement windows with a built-in window seat below which helped with furnishing. A door from the kitchen led to a flat roof which would be enjoyed in warm weather. Two wicker chairs, a card table, a bed and a convertible sofa were all contributed by friends. Marion and Eva splurged and bought a four-dollar chest of drawers. They converted orange crates into stools for dining.

One dollar a day was all that could be allotted for food, so invitations to meals were quickly accepted. When a basket of vegetables and fruit arrived from Morrisburg it was a gala occasion. The two doctors liked to entertain, and their little apartment became a welcome retreat for many friends. Marion's cooking was greatly relished, especially her date bran muffins. As soon as they could afford it, they rented a piano — to Marion, almost a necessity of life.

Complaints occasionally came from the other tenants — but not about Marion's music. What disturbed them was her habit of clattering down the stairs on her frequent night calls. She always apologized and promised to reform; but invariably, in anxiety for her patient, she forgot her good resolutions the very next time she was called out.

The next piece of good fortune to come Marion's way was when a friend gave her a tip on the stock market.

Streetcar at Bay and Adelaide, Toronto, 1927

That tip netted her $500, enough to buy a secondhand Ford. It was her pride and joy. "The streetcars lost a good customer," she later remarked.

In the midst of all her professional activity, she also had a very pleasant social life. During her year abroad she had kept up a correspondence with several men. On her return to Toronto these friendships were renewed. One friend finally outstripped all the other men in his attentions. This attachment ripened until marriage seemed in the offing. A special evening was planned when it was tacitly understood between Marion and her friend that their future together would be discussed. Unfortunately, Marion had just spent three nights in the delivery room and much to the dismay of her friend she fell asleep in his car. This he could not forgive. So faded Marion's childhood dream of becoming 'a married lady with six children.'

Meanwhile, the family news was good. Mr. Hilliard had been honoured in his appointment first as Assistant, then within a year as Master of Osgoode Hall, Ontario's Supreme Court, a position he retained until his retirement in 1935.

Foster and his wife were missionaries in China and Ruth and her husband lived in New York. Both Helen and Irwin were at university and doing well. Marion was especially proud of Irwin, who had won the Blake Medal for Science, including a scholarship. Now he planned to follow in the footsteps of his sister and enter medical school.

Chapter 5 **The Early Thirties**

How did the Depression affect the community in which you live? This information can be found in the files of the local newspaper in the public library or by interviewing someone who lived through that period.

The Great Depression affected everyone. Conditions in Toronto were bitterly hard. Many people were unemployed or had received cuts in wages. If people were unable to pay their rent they were evicted, and usually doubled up with another family. This made for crowded and often unsanitary living conditions and a rise in illness. Sometimes electric or water services were suspended for non-payment of bills and many people suffered from cold and malnutrition in spite of relief money. Such historic buildings as the old St. Lawrence Hall were turned into soup kitchens to feed the hungry.

By now Marion and Eva shared an office with two other physicians, Dr. Gwen Mulock and Dr. Marjorie McIntyre, and a nurse-secretary, Mrs. DeGuchy, in the

The Depression in Toronto — four to a bed

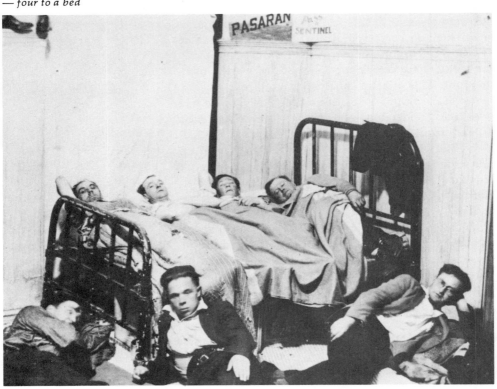

Physicians and Surgeons Building. Their office hours were not supposed to overlap but somehow they did, and the waiting room was often crowded to the doors with the growing practice of each physician.

At this time, out-patient clinics in connection with Women's College Hospital were established for the treatment of needy people. Marion was called upon to handle the obstetrical cases while Eva, newly appointed to the hospital staff, looked after the medical and Dr. Edna Guest the VD patients.

Unemployed men on a protest march, 1930

Ailments which could be treated by household remedies did not come under the scheme for free treatment at clinics. When medications were secured from the relief office the cost was deducted from the sick person's food voucher. Because of this, many people did not turn up at the clinic until their condition had worsened considerably. Hospital treatment depended on the availability of beds in the overcrowded free wards or on charitable agency services.

Only recipients of relief were entitled to visit the clinics. Transients and families not on relief were ineligible, even if they were unable to pay medical bills.

The clinics were terribly crowded. Marion often saw as many as sixty patients in a day, which made for very long working hours in addition to her private practice. Yet the remuneration for this work was very small. A flat scale of fees had been approved by the authorities and was set at $2.00 for an office visit, $3.00 for a house call and $25.00 for maternity care. Every month each doctor billed the province for services rendered to needy patients. When the account had been passed, it was rarely paid in full but only in proportion to the total funds available. Sometimes this was as little as one-half the billing. No matter how much service was given, no doctor got rich in this kind of practice.

Only a few Canadians in the 1930s believed that medical and hospital care should be a government responsibility. Why were so many opposed? What is the role of government in this area today?

Volunteer services were badly needed in many fields. Marion's contribution was to help in planning special programs for girls at the Y.W.C.A. Many of the members were earning low wages or were unemployed. Their outlook was bleak and they were badly in need of recreation to help get through the hard times. Through Marion's efforts, the club dues were reduced for industrial workers, the gym kept open for longer periods, and use of the swimming pool was extended to black women. She herself conducted a Bible study group and helped with educational evenings.

Despite her exhausting work days and volunteer activities, Marion made time for some recreation. In winter, she skated out of doors whenever she could, went to concerts and attended hockey games. Maple Leaf Gardens had just been opened and no one was a greater fan of the Leafs than Marion. She jokingly complained that although she had delivered a baby for the family

of Foster Hewitt, the sportscaster, she was never able
to get season tickets to the games.

Opening night at the Gardens. How was it possible to construct such an expensive building during the Depression?

In summer, she liked to picnic. On one of these
outings she found a delightful spot in Scarborough
overlooking the bluffs and Lake Ontario which she was
able to buy with the help of a loan from an uncle. Here
a simple cottage was built and the property named
Birch Point. Steps down to the beach were cut so that
swimming could be enjoyed, and the telephone company
installed a bell outside the cottage so the hospital could
keep in touch.

At this time the hospital was very shorthanded and
lacking in equipment. An outbreak of diphtheria almost
caused a panic and kept the staff on the jump for weeks.
Later there was a heartbreaking epidemic of childbed
fever. This left Marion with the determination to help
raise standards so that her hospital could minimize
maternal and infant mortality or wipe it out entirely.

In spite of her obvious capabilities, Marion's personality was not always appreciated by some members
of the hospital staff. In their view she bounced, danced,
skated through life and her exuberance was sometimes
hard to take for those of a more quiet disposition. Her

deeper feelings were not always apparent, such as her anguish when a child was stillborn. She had to be strong and would give comfort to the parents and a gentle encouragement to try again. Whatever was going on inside her, she tried to keep up a cheerful and positive attitude.

Possibly the blackest period in her career was when she delivered nine babies in succession, all of whom were abnormal in some way. After the ninth such case she finally broke down and could hardly be comforted. The hospital staff were also horrified by this bad luck. They had never seen Marion so depressed. All perked up when the tenth delivery produced a normal boy.

One of her greatest joys in these hard, busy days was her close association and friendship with her anaesthetist, Dr. Ellen Blatchford. Ellen too had great admiration for Marion. To Ellen, Marion's gentle, swift dexterity in the handling of a birth was almost awe-inspiring. Ellen also admired Marion's sensitive

Ellen Blatchford

understanding of her patient's emotional needs and her reassuring manner.

These two, Marion and Ellen, made a remarkable medical team. Marion was lively and objective, Ellen, quiet, pensive. Each had a strong personality but had the utmost faith in the judgement of the other. They had an arrangement with the hospital that on night calls, both were alerted. Ellen would pick up Marion in her car on the way to the hospital. Marion called Ellen "my favourite night rider," and later gave her an engraved silver box bearing that inscription, one of Ellen's cherished possessions.

After a strenuous five years in hospital and clinic Marion and her chief, Dr. Marion Kerr, arranged for three months' leave of absence so they could go to Europe for further study. They sailed from New York on June 1, 1934, heading for Budapest, where Dr. Kerr was to attend a school of midwifery.

Marion enrolled at the Polyklinic, albeit with great difficulty. In Europe Marion is a boy's name unless it is spelled "Marian," and her application had been accepted as coming from a man. The hospital was not prepared to accept a woman on its staff. They insisted they would refund her registration fee. It was suggested she go elsewhere and study nutrition, a more fitting subject for a woman.

Marion stood by her guns. With great difficulty she persuaded the professor to let her take the course. Later on he came to appreciate her abilities and was kind to her. In the end, the calibre of her work won the admiration not only of her teacher but that of other enrollees from many countries. She was invited to stay on for an extra month. However, she and Dr. Kerr had arranged to visit hospitals in Vienna, then do some work with Miss Dearnley in London on the way home.

Chapter 6 **The New Hospital**

On returning to Toronto, Doctors Kerr and Hilliard found that much progress had been made on the new Women's College Hospital building on Grenville Street. It stood ten storeys high, and had 140 beds. Both doctors had worked very hard for this in a fund-raising campaign waged over several years. In spite of the Depression, some of the senior medical staff had even mortgaged their homes in order to make substantial contributions.

The acknowledged founder of Women's College Hospital was Dr. Augusta Stowe-Gullen, who in 1883, was also the first Canadian woman to receive a medical degree in Canada.

Augusta Stowe-Gullen

Augusta Stowe was the remarkable daughter of an even more remarkable mother, Dr. Emily Howard Jennings Stowe. When her husband became ill and Emily was faced with the necessity of supporting her family, she taught school until she had saved sufficient funds to enable her to enrol in the New York Medical College for Women. She had been refused admittance to the Medical School in Toronto.

She graduated in 1867, returned to Canada and moved her family to Toronto to open an office although she was not licensed to practice in Ontario. It was not until the early 1870's that she was permitted to attend lectures at the Toronto School of Medicine, the first step in obtaining a license. For Emily Stowe and the one other female student, Jennie Trout, the sessions were made as distasteful as possible by some lecturers and many of the male students, but the women stuck it out.

Both Emily and her daughter Augusta were ardent suffragettes and were active in working toward that day in 1918 when Canadian women were finally given the federal vote. Emily never saw that day. She died in 1903, after a lifetime of fighting for her beliefs.

Immediately after her graduation in 1883, Augusta Stowe married a classmate, Dr. John B. Gullen, and was appointed Demonstrator of Anatomy at the Women's Medical College opened that year in Toronto largely at her mother's instigation. She also helped her husband in the establishment of Toronto Western Hospital.

The idea of women in medicine was no longer quite so alarming. Many women were only too pleased to consult a woman doctor. Yet most men and many women still harped on the desirable trait of modesty in women and the disgust aroused at the thought of young men and women dissecting a cadaver together or discussing the grosser physical aspects of life.

Now at last women could study to become doctors without being persecuted, and in an all-female atmosphere. Women's Medical College qualified more than 100 doctors before closing its doors in 1906, when the University of Toronto agreed to accept women.

Alongside the Women's Medical College a clinic for women had been opened in 1888 which operated until 1910. In that year, a house was purchased on Seaton Street for the Women's College Hospital. In 1915 this

Emily Stowe. Name some other Canadian suffragettes.

Women's College Hospital, Seaton Street

Students and faculty of Women's Medical College, 1891-2. Dr. Stowe-Gullen is second from the left in the bottom row.

was exchanged for a house on Rusholme Road, which was used for the next twenty years. It was there that Marion served during the first seven years of her practice and where she was named assistant to Dr. Kerr, the head of the obstetrical department.

Now, on January 22, 1936, the brand-new hospital on Grenville Street was formally opened. The corner stone had been laid earlier by the Prime Minister of Canada, the Honourable R. B. Bennett. He paid tribute to Canadian women for "this monument of their courage, vision and hope." A copper box placed in the cornerstone contained a history of the hospital's ancestor, the Women's Medical College, written by Dr. Augusta Stowe-Gullen. A portrait of this highly respected physician graces the foyer of the hospital to this day.

How Marion rejoiced in the modern facilities and equipment of the new hospital! Her brisk, distinctive

*The Hospital's home on
Rusholme Road*

footsteps could be heard along the corridors of the
obstetrical wing each morning. Patients in wards and
in private rooms listened eagerly for that sound and
faces brightened as it came closer. Everyone on the floor
knew that Dr. Marion Hilliard was on her rounds,
including the nurses, to whom she was known as a strict
disciplinarian when it came to medical protocol and
the nursing care of her patients.

Marion seemed to elicit the utmost confidence from
her patients. Twenty-five years after her death her
name is mentioned and many women smile and remark,
"I'd trust her with my life." Many of them did.

One former patient laughs when she recalls how
after a difficult delivery, following which twenty-five
stitches were required, the doctor patted her shoulder
and remarked, "Best piece of feather-stitching I've ever
done!" This not only comforted the patient but even
brought forth a little grin at a difficult moment. Marion's
special kind of suturing was often referred to by her
confrères as "the Hilliard stitch."

These were exciting times. There were some temporary bright spots in the economy of the country, to the relief of many, and also many stirring events.

The Moose River Mine disaster with its dramatic rescue kept many people glued to their radios for days on end. In May, King George V died and was succeeded by Edward VIII, who six months later dramatically abdicated to marry "the woman I love." A gradual mood of apprehension began to develop with the rise to power of Adolf Hitler in Germany, and Toronto celebrated its centennial, though somewhat modestly in view of the continuing depression.

A prolonged heat wave caused the collapse of many people and families left their stifling homes and crowded Sunnyside and the Exhibition grounds to sleep, hoping for a cool breeze off Lake Ontario.

Birch Point became more and more important to Marion. By now she was occupying an apartment on Clifton Road, looked after by her good friend Mrs. Paterson. Coming home after a tiring day Marion wrote, "The gentle radiance in my livingroom uplifts my heart and dispels my fatigue." Mrs. Paterson recalls Marion once complimenting her by saying, "I couldn't do what

Rescue at Moose River, 1936

you do." Mrs. Paterson modestly replied, "And I couldn't do what you do." It brought smiles from them both.

During the heat wave, however, Marion spent every evening and weekend at Birch Point. To cast off her shoes and stockings and run over the grass in the cool breeze of the lake was her delight. And always she checked on the progress of her garden.

A landscape gardener, the husband of a patient, had carefully planned the planting and was known to say that Marion's garden was the highlight of his career. He always insisted that Marion and he had much in common, she with bringing human life to flower, he with bringing new life from the earth.

Dr. Ellen Blatchford's home was quite near Birch Point and they did much entertaining together. Each summer a picnic for the nursing staff was planned and an annual children's party for Marion's namesakes — of whom there were many. Marion would often invite guests for weekends, and all would turn out to help with setting out plants or weeding.

Birch Point soon became a favourite place to hold wedding receptions, the first of these being that of Marion's younger sister Barby (Helen Barbara) to

The wedding of Helen Barbara Hilliard, 1938

Dr. Burdett McNeel, a classmate and friend of Irwin's.

About this time Marion and the faithful Mrs. DeGuchy moved to an office in the Medical Arts Building where private patients came for treatment. About 40 patients passed in and out of this office each afternoon.

A visit to Marion's office seemed to send women home with an uplifted heart. She didn't give advice or preach to them. What she did was listen. When the patient had spilled out all that was troubling her the troubles seemed to vanish, mainly because she now understood herself better. Marion was often serious and frankly laid down the law on occasion, but she could also be cheerful and help a patient regain her good humour. Always she was forthright and helpful.

She even achieved a certain rapport with men who were the husbands of her patients once their antipathy towards women doctors in general was overcome. And many of them originally had felt this antipathy. Today more than one father will still confess that he would never have survived the ordeal of his wife's first pregnancy had it not been for Dr. Hilliard, who taught him what to expect and how to cope in various situations.

Marion always gave thought to fatherly feelings. She took great delight in announcing a birth herself. Once she called a grandfather by mistake. When she gaily told him, "You have a lovely baby boy," he replied, "I know, I've had him for forty years now." A waiting room for fathers was finally established in the hospital, over considerable objection, but proved a great success. Marion did rule out, however, the presence of fathers in the delivery room after one experiment when the man fainted.

The War Years Chapter 7

Gloom and apprehension seemed to be the general feeling of Canadians at the end of 1938. The depression had worsened and war seemed imminent. Then, in the spring of 1939, King George VI and Queen Elizabeth visited Canada and the situation seemed a little brighter.

It was not to last. The next six years of Marion's life were to be harder on her than any others.

When war broke out, three of Marion's colleagues from Women's College Hospital enlisted. That added greatly to the workload of the remaining doctors. Then it was learned that no woman could legally be commissioned in any of Canada's armed forces, in spite of the services rendered by women in the First World War. This made for an intolerable situation and the Federation of Medical Women of Canada, of which Marion was a member, were up in arms.

If you were a member of the Federation of Medical Women of Canada, how would you present this case to the government?

The Royal Couple in Ottawa, 1939

This organization's early purpose was to act as a guardian for Canadian medical women and to provide scholarships for promising female students. Now, however, the Federation went into high gear.

By 1942 an Act of Parliament was passed permitting the commissioning of women — but with certain restrictions. Women doctors were expected to serve only with women's forces, acting as assistants to male physicians. They would be of lower rank and certainly receive lower pay. To the Federation this was quite out of the question.

The brigadier assigned to hear the petition of the Federation was faced with such a strong committee there was no question as to his decision. From then on enlisted women physicians were entitled to equal rank and pay with male physicians. So it came about that 79 women joined the Royal Canadian Army Medical Corps, 14 the Royal Canadian Air Force and 7 the Royal Canadian Navy, where they would work with both men and women.

Considering the number of male physicians who

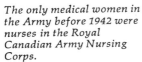

The only medical women in the Army before 1942 were nurses in the Royal Canadian Army Nursing Corps.

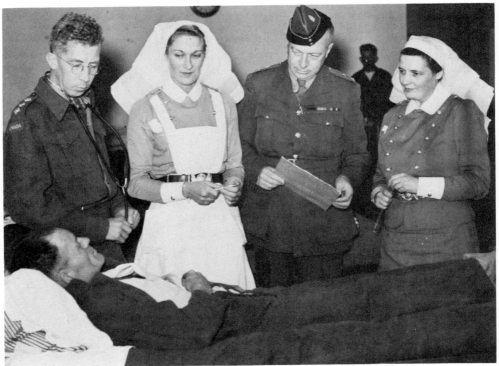

enlisted, this greatly depleted the number of doctors available to serve the civilian population. Marion and her colleagues were kept extremely busy.

What is the ratio of male to female doctors in Canada's armed forces today? Do males and females receive the same wages?

So many of Marion's family now seemed far away. Her parents were now back in Morrisburg following Mr. Hilliard's retirement from Osgoode Hall. He was again practicing law and both were still active in church work. Marion drove down to visit them as often as possible, but it was not like having them close at hand.

Foster, Marion's elder brother, had returned from China some years earlier and taken a degree in divinity. Now he was posted to Trinidad under the auspices of the United Church of Canada. His son, Joe, enlisted in the R.C.A.F.

Word came from brother Irwin in China that he had been appointed chief of a Canadian Missionary Hospital which had already been subjected to Japanese air raids. Irwin cheerfully reported they had a good air raid shelter.

Her sister, Ruth, was still living in New York while her husband, Wentworth Myers, had enlisted in the American Air Force. He was shortly sent to China.

Helen Barbara's husband, Dr. McNeel, joined the Army Medical Corps and was posted to England after training in the Maritimes. Barby lived in Toronto with her two little girls and kept in close touch with Marion.

News of invasions and bombings heightened the tensions of each day. Marion also worried about her many friends in England, especially Mike and Maryon Pearson, as Mike was now stationed there as first secretary to the Canadian High Commissioner, The Honorable Vincent Massey.

The hospital Governors decided there would be no permanent appointments of women of military age. The Medical Advisory Board, of which Marion was a member, found that many staff members had to work on two services to keep all services covered. Marion was also a member of the very busy committee set up by the University of Toronto for British Overseas Children. She was constantly on the go. Once, for a period of nearly two weeks, she never went to bed at all, visiting her apartment only to change her clothes and catching catnaps in her office or the doctors' lounge at the hospital.

A record-breaking blizzard one winter made life

even more difficult. It brought transportation to a standstill. A baby was expected at the hospital and Marion was called at three o'clock in the morning. There was nothing to do but walk the entire twenty blocks in the waist-deep snow. She made it and safely delivered her patient, after which she and the night nurses set up coffee and sandwiches for the staff who straggled in later. Dr. Elizabeth Wiley was greeted with rousing cheers when she arrived on skis.

All this overwork and strain finally took its toll of Marion's usually strong constitution. For the first time in her life she needed medical attention. First she had a small lump in one breast. Then her thyroid gave trouble and a year or two later she required a hysterectomy. Always putting up a brave front, she remarked humourously of herself: "Some people grow viruses, I grow lumps."

At least one good thing came out of this. Marion was ordered to take a vacation. It was her first in a long time. Midway through the war she had met Opal Boynton through some mutual social-work friends. Poppy, as she was nicknamed, was a New Yorker, a sports enthusiast with a gusty humour. When she found that Marion had never been trout fishing, she arranged to meet her for a holiday at her favourite fishing camp in Laurentide Park, a hundred miles north of Quebec City.

Drowsing in a boat while trolling on the calm waters of the lake and breathing the pine-scented northern air restored not only Marion's weakened body but also her strength of spirit. Health improved, she donned waders and attempted the turbulent trout streams. Sportswoman that she was, it was not long before she had learned the finer points of trout fishing and was able to compete with the experts for the "best catch of the day." Her friends recall with glee the evening when an announcement was made that Dr. Hilliard's catch would be displayed. Someone produced a very small minnow on a very large platter, to the amusement of all present, including Marion.

Poppy, too, was war-weary, having been on the move for more than four years as a program director for the USO. As the two of them enjoyed subsequent fishing trips together, their friendship deepened. Finally Marion asked Poppy what she wanted to do after the

Marion on a fishing
excursion in Quebec, 1945

war. The prompt reply was that she wanted to live in
the country and raise bees. "What a gorgeous idea!"
was Marion's reaction. "There is a property adjoining
mine at Scarborough that would be ideal for such a
project. Why not join me there?" But of course, this
would have to wait.

In August of 1945 there was great excitement in the
fishing camp but the only English-speaking member of
the staff happened to be absent. So it was not until the
following day on their way back to Toronto that Marion
and Poppy learned of the bombing of Hiroshima. A
few days later bells rang and whistles blew as everyone
celebrated V-J Day.

Before the year was out all the members of the Hilliard
clan returned safe and sound. A joyful if brief reunion
was held at Irwanna before their return to peacetime
occupations.

Chapter 8 **Bees In Her Bonnet**

The bee farm at Birch Point

Birch Point literally became a hive of activity after the war. Poppy moved in with Marion and they began their bee farm. First they bought only 10 hives but these soon grew to 60. A honey house was built and a part time bee-master, Mr. Horne, was engaged to help with the work. The yield was usually 40 kg of honey from each hive, a total of 2400 kg, as well as 125 comb sections. Not only were all their friends supplied with honey but Dom and Tony, who ran a local grocery store, used to market it for them. One of Marion's biggest thrills was to turn the handle of the honey extractor and see the fruit of her work pouring out in a golden stream.

In addition to their mutual interest in bees, sports and music, both Marion and Poppy were deeply religious. Together they were confirmed and became members of the Church of the Holy Trinity, where Canon John Frank ministered to rich and poor alike. Marion had been brought up on the Bible and, true to her family training, participated in worship regularly throughout her life. For five years, during the six weeks of Lent, she invited special friends to her home for prayer and Bible study. This was an enriching experience to all who attended.

Significant of the continuing accord between Marion and her friend Ellen Blatchford was the occasion when, at one of these informal religious discussions, someone expressed a doubt of miracles. Almost as one Marion

Marion, Jessie Gray, and Poppy Boynton

and Ellen replied, "You can't be a doctor and not believe in miracles. We've seen them happen."

To many people Marion seemed very ebullient — always boiling with enthusiasms and opinions. She *was* ebullient but she was also steady and she had a true humility of heart. Once when she appeared on a radio program with Canon Frank she said: "My private prayers are really not for publication. I'm afraid I have my own language. One prayer of great significance to me came to me once as I sat in my own church. It was this: 'O, Lord, I think I talk too much and write too much and if I am not careful I will be a windbag. O, Lord, help me to be an instrument and not a windbag.' "

Besides her busy practice and her life at Birch Point Marion had other "bees in her bonnet." She was an innovator. She was bursting with ideas as to how the services of the hospital could be expanded or improved. Often she had to talk her way through indifference and resistance until others took an interest in her plans. Even then, when one of her suggestions was put to a vote, reactionaries on the staff outvoted her, and this happened more than once. One of Marion's ardent hopes was that the hospital would become accepted for teaching by the University's Faculty of Medicine. The Board of Governors also favoured this. When Marion's name was proposed as chairman of the Medical Advisory Board, others on the staff persuaded a doctor with opposite views to stand for election and packed the meeting so that Marion was defeated.

It was difficult to accept this and other similar verdicts gracefully but, good sport that she was, Marion did. Few people knew that sometimes she went home and cried in frustration. The time would come, however, when her achievements, hard come by as they were, would add greatly to the fame and status of Women's College Hospital.

In 1947, Dr. Kerr resigned and Marion was appointed her successor as head of the gynecology and obstetrics department. This was a responsible position that fully occupied her time. It also required her supervision of younger and less experienced doctors. She cheerfully accepted this and found the experience valuable.

Another of Marion's "bees" was her dream of establishing a cancer detection clinic for women. As usual, she encountered opposition and diffidence. Some thought it would be a waste of time. Others argued that it might give the patients a false sense of security. There were worries that it would take patients away from private physicians. And there were those who warned that it would take a lot of money and professional time to discover just a few cancer cases.

Marion countered, "It would be worthwhile if it were only half of one percent."

Where was the money to come from? Here again Marion's determination and ingenuity became apparent. She heard that a Canadian brewing company had offered a sizeable donation to the United Church of Canada. It had been declined because of its source. She thought, "Why don't we go after that money?" After consultation with the Board of Governors she did, and a substantial donation resulted. Teasing about this came in the form of a squib in a magazine: "What doctor from what famous temperance family was recently instrumental in getting money from a beer company for her hospital?"

Marion laughed. The money was needed and would be put to good use, so why quibble?

The Soroptimist Club of Toronto, whose major service project at the time was cancer care for women, were delighted to furnish the new clinic. They established an annual grant for refurbishing to honour one of their members who had served for many years on the hospital's Board of Governors.

The big day arrived on April 7, 1948, when Marion cut the ribbon to open the new clinic, the first of its kind in Canada. Dr. Elise L'Esperance from the Strang Memorial Cancer Prevention Clinic of New York, a friend of long standing, was guest of honour. That evening she delivered a lecture to mark the occasion. Later, an article of Marion's describing an improved method of cancer detection developed in the clinic bought enquiries from all over the world.

When the time came to think of further hospital

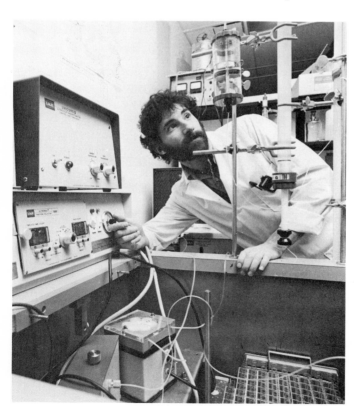

Modern cancer research at McMaster University

expansion Marion had another bright idea — a radio broadcast of the birth of a baby to interest the general public in making donations. Scandal almost resulted. Hundreds of telephone calls were received at the hospital, expressing either high approval or the exact opposite. Letters to the CBC also showed great extremes in reaction.

The headmistress of a girls' school invited Marion to speak at a special evening program and present the tape. The girls responded to her sparkling personality and the adults present felt that "her wholesome approach to sex was like a fresh, clean breeze." The girls were absolutely spellbound by the tape. There was no giggling or laughing. All were caught up in an atmosphere of awe and wonder. It was evident that what they had previously heard about birth had made them think it was just an unrewarding, painful experience women had to go through. They were shocked that so many people had been critical of the broadcast.

The Fifties Chapter 9

A great tragedy occurred in the Hilliard family in the
fall of 1949. Two years earlier, Marion had purchased a
house on Lonsdale Road in Toronto for her aging parents.
They had settled there happily. Mr. Hilliard, in his late
eighties, had become very frail and forgetful. He had
wandered away several times but had always found
his way home. Now he was missing and could not be
found. Friends, neighbours and the police in helicopters
and on foot conducted a search for nineteen days until
his body was discovered in a ravine where he apparently
had sat down to rest before death overtook him. It made
for a very sad family Christmas that year.

Marion's health now seemed completely restored.
A friend remarked to her, "I saw you grow old during
the war, now you seem young again." She was working
hard, and with renewed energy. It was conceded that

*A family gathering for Anna
Hilliard's eightieth birthday.
Marion is standing behind
her mother.*

Marion's obstetrical practice was the largest in Toronto.
Some months she delivered as many as forty babies. With
her supervisory work at the hospital this was a heavy
workload, and she began to cut down. Male obstetricians
would have been glad to have some of her referrals,
but Marion preferred to make these to topnotch women
specialists or to help some younger women obstetricians
build their practices. She contended that no man had
helped her to get started and that to get anywhere in
the medical profession a woman had to be about 25%
better than her male competitors.

A dream that Marion had had for a long time now
came true. She was finally able to afford an all-year-round
house at Birch Point and give up her city apartment.
How she appreciated the perfection of the new house!
And the gardens now were a picture all year round.
First there were snowdrops, daffodils, hyacinths and
tulips, then petunias, lobelias, snapdragons, phlox and
Marion's favourite blue delphiniums all summer long. In
autumn, marigolds and chysanthemums bloomed in
profusion. A blue spruce tree, an early gift from Marion's
father, was a special favourite. It stood outside the
picture window and was gaily decorated at Christmas.

By now Marion had acquired ten nieces and nephews
over a period of nineteen years and they were among
her favourite guests. They all adored her and she not
only dreamed affectionately of the good life for them
but felt she learned much from the younger generation.

A presentation to honour Marion at the culmination
of her career took place at the Royal York Hotel in
January of 1956. So many of her patients were ap-
preciative not only of the service she had given them
but of her generous sharing of her philosophy of life
that they established a fund in her name to be applied
to any medical project she might designate. Her oldest
friends, Lester ("Mike") Pearson, now Secretary of
State, and Maryon Pearson were invited, and they even
participated in a hula dance as part of the floor show.
Mrs. Pearson made the presentation in a witty little
speech referring to her college days with Marion, and
told of how Marion had helped her out of a window on
the night of a forbidden dance.

The Trust Company representative presented a
cheque for about seven thousand dollars. Then Mrs.

Pearson presented a large volume bearing the signatures of nearly eleven hundred patient contributors. Mrs. Pearson read the dedication page:

To Marion Hilliard, Physician and Friend.
Whose skillful hands have been the world's first sure strong cradle for thousands of new babies born in her care. Whose understanding, yet challenging voice has spoken wise counsel, replacing ignorance with knowledge, and fear with courage, for thousands of women who have been her patients.

Whose love of life and of her God has been her freely communicated gift to the men and women of her church, her community and her world.

Work on the fund-raising campaign for the hospital was continuing and a new idea was put to Marion. The husband of one of her patients suggested that she write a series of articles for *Chatelaine*. A handsome fee would be paid. She protested she had no time, then realized that this too could be a source of funds for the hospital. By now she was so accustomed to lecturing that she decided to use a tape recorder as her method of authorship and over a period of several years this proved to be a great success. Some of her topics were "Woman's Greatest Hazard — Sex", "Dr. Hilliard Talks to Single Women", "Don't be Afraid of Growing Old" and "The Four Main Fears of Women". So the series grew.

These articles almost raised another scandal. "What does *she* know about marriage?" more than one person scoffed. Marion herself felt that she knew hundreds of marriages through her patients, while most women knew only one, their own.

The most adverse reaction came from some of her medical colleagues. They somehow got the idea that Marion's motive was to advertise her obstetrical and marriage counselling services. They little knew that Marion was already cutting down her practice and no such publicity could possibly be in her mind. Her friends also scoffed at the suggestion, saying "Just try to get an appointment with her these days!" Marion herself said, "All I wanted was to help people understand themselves a little better. If I have achieved that, to even the smallest degree, I am happy." And the proceeds from these articles did provide a substantial donation to the campaign fund.

Many of her former patients sent donations to the fund. One sent in a contribution with a note saying, "But for Dr. Hilliard's care, I shouldn't be the lusty 79-year-old person I happily am."

Marion was interviewed on television on behalf of the hospital fund-raising campaign. She was also instrumental in having televised a series of tapes for teaching trainees the techniques required in the practice of obstetrics.

Finally, again over many objections, Marion was successful in having Women's College Hospital accepted in 1956 as a teaching hospital by the University of Toronto, her own department being the first so designated. Her outstanding ability and dedication to the teaching of her profession is clearly demonstrated in the account she wrote of one of her students.

"I've been packing up my private practice gradually over the past three years, passing it along to younger women of miraculous competence and confidence. I watched one of them deliver a baby only a few days ago. She's a Japanese-Canadian, small and fragile and possessed of magnificent sensitivity in a delivery room. I felt choked by strong emotion in that moment, and movement in the room seemed to stop as in a tableau. I knew a giddy pride in my profession, in my sex, and in myself. There was a blessedness in the room — the woman on the delivery table with the beginning of glory in her face, the tiny doctor holding the new infant with skill and affection, the first raw sound of a cry. I thought of my twenty-five years in this room and others like it, less well equipped. I stood tall and felt strong because I am comfortable with my no-longer young body and my conscience treats me benignly."

It was on a glorious autumn day in 1956 that the new hospital wing and nurses' residence were formally opened. Burton Hall, named after the campaign chairman, could accommodate 200 nurses and housed the nurses' training school. Over 150 beds were added in the new wing of the hospital along with 100 bassinets. One old-fashioned note was preserved in the new modern setting — the rocking chairs where nurses sat to feed the "bottle babies."

The Right Honourable Louis St. Laurent, then Prime Minister of Canada, cut the ribbon to formally open the new wing, and among the many other notables present

Women's College Hospital
today

sat the beaming figure of Dr. Marion Hilliard, thoroughly
enjoying the climax of her long and arduous campaign.

The articles Marion had written for *Chatelaine* came
out in book form in June, 1957, under the title *A Woman
Doctor Looks at Love and Life*. Marion's picture was
widely publicized, which rather dismayed her, but she
delighted in the numerous letters which her book stimu-
lated former patients and friends to write from far and
near. She also received many letters from doctors, nurses,
librarians and psychologists, telling her how helpful her
book was in their own practices.

That same month began the series of parties given
in her honour, to commemorate her retirement as chief
of obstetrics at Women's College Hospital. When the
hospital's Board of Governors presented her with a silver
coffee set she made a very humorous speech, poking fun

at herself for the furore she had caused within the hospital from time to time. Later she wrote, "I can never express in words my feelings about the Board. They have made it possible for me to work out my whole life's salvation."

Dr. Hilliard at a retirement banquet

Dreams, Faith and Reality

Chapter 10

Marion's first book ended with the words, "I am starting
a new life soon. Wish something with me. Wish that it
will be difficult. And full of laughter."

At age 55 Marion had many dreams for her new life.
Could she now fulfill her girlhood dreams of helping
in the pioneer work of women doctors in India, Japan
or China? This would follow in the footsteps of her
two brothers who had served in mission fields abroad.
She wanted to spend a year in Greece or Turkey. She
longed to hear opera in Milan or go salmon fishing in
British Columbia. She could hardly wait to get at the
future.

At first she was busy preparing lectures and travelling
to speak at various medical gatherings. She was asked to
write an article for a prominent women's magazine in the
United States under the title, "Why Premarital Sex is
Always Wrong." She refused. To her this title was
too 'black and white'. Instead, she wrote an article titled
"Modern Variations on the Ancient Theme of Passion,"
which delighted the editor and her readers.

In 1955-6 Marion had served as president of the
Federation of Medical Women of Canada. Now she was
slated to become president of the International Medical
Women's Association, a very high honour. She planned
to visit England in the following July to be installed
at the annual meeting of the Association. There was
certainly lots to do.

In an address given to a graduating class of nurses,
she attempted to sort out for them her philosophy of life.
She said in part, "First, I have no faith in the fairness
of life. There is no balance or reward for effort or happiness for a kind heart. There is rarely even gratitude.
No one can expect that life will be gracious and filled
with esteem for the mere reason of worthiness. You
don't get out of living what you deserve. Since it is
impossible for even the most saintly to live without

Marion at a nurses' graduation

misfortune, the hope for the serene survival of the spirit is acceptance.

"I don't mean the passive, heavy acceptance called fatalism. This is far too inert for me. I believe that living is too important, too highly charged with potential, to be derailed by a brutal kick from fate. There's laughter going on, and hard work, and the occasional rocket of worth-while achievement slashing the darkness. The immobility of self-pity is a kind of death, a suicide.

"I believe in timing. It is crystallized for me in the moment of greatness that an athlete like Mickey Mantle knows for that fraction of time when his bat meets the ball squarely and sends it out of the park. This is true timing — the health and animal instinct of a superb athlete performing perfectly at the time and place best suited to him.

"All individuals must find this kind of timing. This timing process can't be rushed or the whole pattern of a life is jostled. It must be taken with fluid grace, one step at a time. This is the beginning of wisdom.

"Timing has its own rhythm. In each life there is a time, clearly defined by nature in the extra vigor of the young, for striving and ambition; there is an ebb time for tranquillity. There is a time for passion and a time for contentment. The reckless ones who try to jar the rhythm and look for peace when it is too soon, or accomplishment when it is too late can only be shattered.

"Life holds one certain quality for everyone — suffering. This is to be expected. The extra bonus that life sometimes gives is achievement. I would never wish anyone a life of prosperity and security. These are bound to betray. I would wish instead for adventure, struggle and challenge. These have one benefit in common — they require a pinnacle of effort, the very best. Nothing in life is as glorious as reaching beyond capacity."

In the midst of Marion's plans for her future career she began to feel tired and run down. A holiday in Jamaica did no good. She consulted her friend, Dr. Jean Davey, and learned to take the advice she had so often prescribed — more rest. It was thought at first that she had virus pneumonia. Then there was a suspicion of cancer but no proof. Finally, for the first time in her life, she had to cancel her plans because of poor health. She was both puzzled and frightened at the way her dependable, robust constitution was letting her down.

In the spring of 1958 Marion once again enjoyed the gardens at Birch Point, the cherry trees and forsythia in bloom, the first shy violets and the warmth of the sun. But her symptoms became more serious. She became gray in the face and had a deeply wracking cough. She was too good a clinician not to be aware of these symptoms, and now she bravely entered into her 'ebb time of tranquillity.'

She would lie in the garden and watch her spaniel "Ginny" chase her shadow, although she no longer had the strength to run and play with her. Her house was filled with music and there was much lighthearted conversation with the close friends who visited her.

Although, on orders of Dr. Davey, she had to rest a lot, she also accomplished much work. A friend of long standing, Marion Robinson of New York, came to stay, and together they worked on a new book, *Women and Fatigue*, requested by her publisher.

She taped a radio interview which was to be broadcast in four parts. The final broadcast was the only one she herself listened to because she was not sure whether she had clearly expressed her thoughts. The interviewer had asked her, "As a doctor, are you concerned with the subject of death?"

Marion replied that in her practice she had more to do with the beginning of life than its end, but she had never been afraid of death. In the case of a patient dying of cancer, the doctor did his or her utmost to make the patient comfortable so that the future could be faced with serenity, peace and almost a contentment. She continued: "I may have a different feeling about death from what some people have. I never worry about the person who is dying. I only worry about the ones who are left behind . . . I think the person who is going on can often comfort the ones who are going to stay."

After the broadcast Marion said quietly, "Yes, that's what I meant."

A few weeks after her 56th birthday in June, Marion suffered a partial lung collapse and required hospitalization so oxygen could be administered. Typical of her continued zest for life was her enjoyment of her first ever ambulance trip. Sirens screaming, they disrupted the annual Orangemen's parade. "At last I'm having my innings with those boys. For years I've been held up by that darned parade," she joked.

When Marion was made comfortable in her oxygen tent, her brother Irwin and her closest friends spelled each other out over these last few days so she was never left alone. She was cheerful in her waking hours and gaily asked everyone to do things for her so they would feel better. She took comfort from the reading by Poppy of the daily lesson from the Anglican prayer book and a visit from her good friend, Canon John Frank.

On Thursday, July 15, 1958, Marion passed away in her sleep. An obscure cancerous growth was only proven by autopsy.

"It's a sad day for Toronto," said an anonymous taxi driver as he heard the news over his radio. His fare, a personal friend of Marion's, was so shaken he dumbly handed the cabby a bill and left the taxi, not trusting himself to speak.

The deep feelings of thousands of women whose lives Marion had touched in her career were expressed in an article by a former patient. After telling of her own experiences as a patient she concluded: "I know that if you could talk to us now you would tell us not to mourn for you. You would tell us briskly to carry on with living . . . I know you are still very much alive in this world. You are living through the thousands of babies you brought into the world and through all the thousands of adults you have influenced, steadied, helped . . . For all you have done for so many of us, I think it will make everyone feel a little comforted if we can say once more . . . Thank you, Dr. Hilliard." The news was carried around the world and tributes began to arrive from far and near.

The funeral service for Marion was held in St. James Cathedral, which was packed to the doors with people from all walks of life. Marion's favourite hymns were sung.

Perhaps the most poignant moment came at the close of the service when the great bell began to toll and the casket was wheeled from the cathedral. Following were the honourary pall bearers, Dr. Evelyn Bateman, Dr. Ellen Blatchford, Dr. Dorothy Daley, Dr. Jean Davey, Dr. Marjorie Davis, Dr. Jessie Gray, Dr. Eva McDonald, Dr. Geraldine Maloney, Dr. Margaret McEachern, Dr. Marjorie McIntyre, Dr. Elizabeth Stewart and Dr. Elizabeth Wiley — Marion's closest friends and colleagues.

At the door the casket was raised shoulder high and carried by Marion's nephews, both real and adopted, to the waiting car.

Marion was buried at Morrisburg. Her headstone bears a simple epitaph: "Beloved Physician."

Interview a woman doctor in your community to learn if it is still true as Marion believed that a woman doctor must be "25% better than her male competitors" to succeed in her profession. Try to find out if this is true in other professions and occupations.

Marion poses for a father with a "Hilliard baby"

Further Reading

Hacker, Carlotta. *The Indomitable Lady Doctors*. Clarke Irwin, 1974.

Hilliard, Marion. *A Woman Doctor Looks at Love and Life*. Doubleday, 1956.

Hilliard, Marion. *Women and Fatigue*. Doubleday, 1960.

Horn, Michael, ed. *The Dirty Thirties*. Copp Clark, 1972.

Robinson, Marion O. *Give My Heart, The Dr. Marion Hilliard Story*. Doubleday, 1964.

West, Bruce. *Toronto*. Doubleday, 1967.

Credits

My grateful thanks to Dr. and Mrs. Irwin Hilliard who checked my manuscript and provided many photographs, to Dr. Ellen Blatchford, Marion's 'favourite night rider,' to Miss Dorothy Macham of Women's College Hospital for providing much useful information, and to the many friends and former patients of Dr. Marion Hilliard who generously shared with me their memories of this beloved physician.

Academy of Medicine, Toronto, pages 36, 38, 40
Canadian Cancer Society, page 51
Dr. Irwin Hilliard, pages 1, 3, 4, 6, 7, 8, 11, 15, 17, 18, 20, 23, 34, 41, 47, 48, 49, 53, 58, 63
Metropolitan Toronto Library Board, pages 8, 12, 33, 37, 39
Public Archives of Canada, pages 13 (C 68799), 25, 27 (C 29449), 30 (C 13236), 31 (C 29397), 43 (C 2179), 44 (DND 7151)
Queen Charlotte Hospital, London, page 21
Rotunda Hospital, Dublin, page 22
Toronto Transit Commission, page 29
United Church Archives, page 26
University of Toronto, page 10
Women's College Hospital, pages 28, 38, 57, 60

Editing: Sheba Meland, Barbara Czarnecki
Design: Jack Steiner
Cover Illustration: Leoung O'Young

The Canadians

Consulting Editor: Roderick Stewart
Editor-in-Chief: Robert Read

Every effort has been made to credit all sources correctly. The author and publishers will welcome any information that will allow them to correct any errors or omissions.